Arcola Theatre presents

Hoard

by **Bim Adewunmi**

GW00671395

Cast

Ami Bakare	**Emmanuella Cole**
Wura Bakare	**Ellen Thomas**
Rafi Bakare	**Elizabeth Ita**
Bili Bakare	**Kemi Durosinmi**
Brian Burton	**Tyler Fayose**

Writer	**Bim Adewunmi**
Director	**Femi Elufowoju jr.**
Costume Designer and Associate Set Design	**Bex Kemp**
Casting Director	**Nadine Rennie CDG**
Stage Manager	**Catriona McHugh**
Sound Designer	**Chris Drohan**
Lighting Designer	**Geoff Hense**

First performed
Wednesday 15 May 2019 | Arcola Theatre, London

Special thanks to

Alan Benton, Almeida Theatre, Rafe Gibbons, Mikaela Knops, Dr Richard Lawson, Dr Claire Lockwood, Joyce Nettles, David C. Northrop, Karina Olsen, Tommy Papaioannou, Jonny Powell, Sebastien Robinson, Laura Rolinson, Radmila Sarac, Ginny Schiller

The Company

Emmanuella Cole
Ami Bakare

Theatre credits include: *An Octoroon* (National Theatre); *Kingdom Come* (RSC); *The Iliad* (Royal Lyceum - Critics Award Nomination for Best Female as Hera); *The Curious Incident of the Dog in the Night Time* (National Theatre - Olivier Award Best New Play); *Revolt. She Said. Revolt Again.* (RSC); *Roadkill* (Traverse Theatre - Olivier Award for Outstanding Achievement in Affiliate Theatre); *But I Cd Only Whisper* (Arcola Theatre); *Danton's Death* (National Theatre); *Dancing Bears* (Soho Theatre); *Faith, Hope and Charity* (Southwark Playhouse); *African Snow* (Trafalgar Studios); *This Wide Night* (Bernie Grant Arts Centre). Television credits include: include *In The Long Run* (Sky One); *Strike - Career of Evil* (HBO/Bronte/BBC); *Obsession* (Discovery USA); *Cucumber* (Channel 4/Red Productions); *Top Boy* (Channel 4); *Scott and Bailey* (ITV/Red Productions); *Law & Order* (ITV/Kudos); *Throne: Sleepyhead* (Sky One); *EastEnders* (BBC One); *Hollyoaks Later* (Channel 4); *Little Miss Jocelyn* (BBC Three/BBC Two).

Ellen Thomas
Wura Bakare

Ellen Thomas is a Sierra Leonian born British actress. Her TV credits include: *EastEnders* (BBC One), *Moses Jones* (BBC One), *Rev* (BBC Two), *The Jury* (BBC One), *Dr Who* (BBC One), *Casualty* (BBC One), *Teachers* (Channel 4), *Midsomer Murders* (ITV), *Humans* (series 1) (Channel 4), *Mount Pleasant* (Sky TV). Theatre Credits Include: *Hotel Cerise* (Theatre Royal Stratford East), *Amen Corner* (Tricycle Theatre), several plays at the Royal National Theatre, several plays at the Royal Court Theatre and several plays at Manchester Royal Exchange Theatre. Film Credits include: *Breaking and Entry*, *Johnny English Reborn*, *Buried Treasure*, *Clubbed*, *Basic Instinct 2*, *The Queen and I*, *Golden Years*.

Elizabeth Ita
Rafi Bakare

Elizabeth won an acting scholarship
and trained for three years at the South
campus of the Academy of Live and
Recorded Arts. Since graduating in 2011
she's made appearances in *Coronation
Street*, *Count Arthur Strong*, *Il Sonnambulo*
and *The Favourite*. Theatre work includes:
Mandela and *Dream Nation* both with
Tangle International Theatre (tour) and *Sum Zero* at the Lyric
Hammersmith.

Kemi Durosinmi
Bili Bakare

Kemi Durosinmi is a Multidisciplinary
Performer and Creative Artist.
Theatre Credits include: *Death & The Kings
Horseman* (National Theatre); *Branded* (Old
Vic); *Thriller Live* (West End). Screen Credits
Include: *Game Of Thrones* (HBO); *Last
Christmas* (Grunewald Films); *Third Sorrow*
(NFTS). Choreography & Movement Direction Credits include:
The Secret Lives Of Baba Segi Wives (Arcola Theatre); *Becoming*
(Stratford Theatre); *Britain's Got Talent* (ITV), *1xtra Live*, Ferrari &
Drive Productions, WOMAD Festival, Zalando, Nike.

Tyler Fayose
Brian Burton

Tyler has performed on many of London's
famous stages including playing Don Pedro
in *Much A Do About Nothing* (2018) and
Lorenzo in T*he Merchant Of Venice* (2014)
both at The Globe Theatre. Tyler has
also worked at Soho Theatre, Southwark
Playhouse, Stratford Theatre Royal, The
Lyric Theatre, Theatre 503, and Cockpit Theatre amongst others.
Tyler has also acted in film and television. He appeared in *Casualty*
(2013), *Mission Impossible: Rogue Nation* (2014), and *Skybound*
(2017). Later in 2019 he will appear in a six-part drama series on
Global TV.

Femi Elufowoju, jr
Director

Femi Elufowoju, jr is an award winning performer-director, freelance producer Radio Drama for the BBC and Creative director of Elufowoju jr Ensemble.

Directing credits include: *Tickets & Ties*, *The Hotel Cerise* (Theatre Royal Stratford East); *Dealer's Choice* (Salisbury Playhouse); *Off Camera*, *Medea* (West Yorkshire Playhouse); *The Big Men* (National Theatre), *Bone* (Royal Court), *Blues for an Alabama Sky* (RADA); *The Gods are not to Blame* and *Blue/Orange* (tiata fahodzi/ Arcola Theatre); Efe Paul Azino's *Finding Home* (Terra Kulture, Lagos & Goethe Institut/Theater Expedition Metropolis Berlin); *Things Fall Apart* (Queen Elizabeth Hall, Southbank Centre); *The Secret Lives of Baba Segi's Wives* an Elufowoju jr Ensemble co-production with Arcola Theatre (for which he won the Best Director Award for an Off-West End play 2019). The production was restaged for Ake Arts and Book Festival in Lagos Nigeria in 2018 (the play's second visit in five years). Femi's recent direction is for the Watford Palace and Arcola Theatre co-production of Tennessee Williams *The Glass Menagerie*.

Femi established the first ever African national touring theatre company in Britain, tiata fahodzi which he led artistically for thirteen years (1997/2010). His penultimate production for the company (Oladipo Agboluaje's *Iya-Ile, the first wife*) was nominated for an Olivier Award. His has since served as Associate Director for Royal Court, West Yorkshire Playhouse, New Wolsey Theatre, Ipswich and as Associate Artist at the Almeida. As a performer on stage, screen and television – he is most noted for his roles in the Bafta award winning series *Borgen* (BBC), the thriller feature film *Mechanic Resurrection*, *The Saint* and the highly successful *Sex Education* (both for Netflix).

Bex Kemp
Associate Set Designer & Costume Designer

Bex is a Set and Costume Designer and Costume Supervisor. She trained at the Royal Central School of Speech and Drama.

Designs include: *F*ck The Polar Bears* (Bush Theatre); *Gracie, Dubailand & Andy Capp The Musical* (Finborough); *West End Bares: Vogue* (Shaftesbury Theatre); *Pint Sized: OctoberFest* (Bunker Theatre); *Becoming Mohammed* (Pleasance Theatre); *All of Me* (Cannes Film Festival); *Everyday People* (Bridewell); *Reunion & Dark Pony* (Site-Specific); *About Miss Julie* (King's Head); *Othello* (Greenwich Theatre/Underbelly); *As You Like It* (UK Tour); *Pentecost, Variations on The Death of Trotsky, Scenes From The Big Picture, Common Chorus & Seventh Continent* (RCSSD); *Nell Gwynn, 1984 & Everyman* (London College of Music); *Kleinkunst 3* (Roundhouse).

Bex is a Design Assistant to Miriam Buether. Other Design Assistance: *Iphigenia Quartet* (Cécile Trémolières/Gate Theatre); *The Bodyguard* (Tim Hatley/Adelphi Theatre); *The Boy Who Climbed Out Of His Face* (Rachel Good/Shunt); *Sleeping Beauty* (Keith Orton/Salisbury Playhouse), *The Duchess of Malfi* (Punchdrunk/ENO).

Catriona McHugh
Designer

Credits as Stage Manager Include: *Hoard* (Arcola Theatre); *Chasing Bono* (Soho Theatre); *Wasted* (Southwark Playhouse); *Spun* (Arcola Theatre); *Lock & Key* (The Vault's Festival 18); *Ad Libido* (The Vault's Festival 18); *Mary's Babies* (The Vault's Festival 18); *Talk Radio* (Old Red Lion Theatre); *Boom* (Theatre 503).

Credit for other roles: *Three Sisters* (Tech Week Runner, Almeida Theatre); *The Writer* (Stage Crew,); *The Twilight Zone* (Tech Week Runner, Almeida Theatre); *Albion* (Assistant Stage Manager, Almeida).

Chris Drohan
Sound Designer

Chris was nominated for the 2017 OffWestEnd Sound Design Award for his work on *Tenderly: The Rosemary Clooney Musical* at the Wimbledon Studio.

Sound Design credits include: *Boots* (The Bunker); *New Nigerians* (Arcola and UK Tour); *The Paradise Circus* (The Playground Theatre); *Clockwork Canaries* (Theatre Royal Plymouth); *After the Ball* (Gatehouse); *All Or Nothing* (Arts Theatre, West End); *Thrown* (Brighton Digital Festival); *9 to 5* (Gatehouse); *Tenderly: The Rosemary Clooney Musical* (Wimbledon Studio); *What Shadows* (Edinburgh Lyceum, as Associate Sound Designer); *Ready Or Not* (UK Tour/Arcola Theatre); *The Mirror Never Lies* (Cockpit); *After Three Sisters* (Jack Studio Theatre); *Tonight at the Museum: Charlie Chaplin* (Cinema Museum); *Tis Pity* (Tristan Bates); *The Pursuit of Happiness* (RADA Festival); *Phoebe* (Kings Head Theatre); *The Marvellous Adventures of Mary Seacole* (Edinburgh Festival); *In The Gut* (Blue Elephant); *All Or Nothing* (Vaults Theatre/UK Tour); *The Lamellar Project* (UK Tour and Arcola Theatre); *Dr. Angelus, Don't Smoke in Bed* and *The One Day of the Year* (Finborough); *Spring Awakening* and *Seussical* (Chelsea Theatre); *Resolution* (The Space/Etcetera Theatre); *The Drunken City* (Tabard Theatre); *Roaring Trade* and *Finders Keepers* (Park Theatre); *Stiching* (White Bear); *Counting Stars* (Old Red Lion/Assembly Edinburgh); *The Social Network* (Lion and Unicorn/ Camden Fringe); *La Boheme* (Arcola Theatre); *Shock Treatment* (Kings Head Theatre).

As a Composer, recent credits include a new score for *The Beggar's Opera* with Bobby Locke at the Jack Studio Theatre, and a BBC Radio Drama Production of *Andromache*.

Geoff Hense
Lighting Designer

Geoff is Head of Production at Arcola Theatre. His recent lighting designs include: *Sitting, Keith, Spun, The Daughter-in-Law* (Arcola); *Byron: Angel and Outcast* (Cadogan Hall); *Secret Life of Humans* (New Diorama/ Edinburgh Festival); *Testosterone* (Edinburgh Festival/International Tour); *64 Squares* (New Diorama / Tour); Richard II (Arcola / UK Parliament).

arcola theatre

Arcola Theatre is one of London's leading off-West End theatres.

Locally engaged and internationally minded, we stage a diverse programme of plays, operas and musicals. New productions from major artists appear alongside cutting-edge work from the most exciting emerging companies.

Every year, our Participation department creates over 13,500 creative opportunities for the people of Hackney and beyond, and 26 weeks of free rehearsal space for theatre artists of colour. Our pioneering environmental initiatives are internationally renowned, and aim to make Arcola the world's first carbon-neutral theatre.

MAKE THIS HAPPEN Text ARCO14 £3 to 70070 to give £3 in support of Arcola  Standard network charges apply.

Artistic Director **Mehmet Ergen**	Executive Producer **Leyla Nazli**		Executive Director **Ben Todd**
Associate Director **Jack Gamble**	Head of Production **Geoff Hense**	Participation Manager **Bec Martin-Williams**	Producer **Richard Speir**
Marketing Manager **Maddy Breen**	Front of House & Box Office Manager **Norna Yau**	Operations Manager **Natalja Derendiajeva**	Bar Manager **Shanker Krishnan**
Finance Assistant **Steve Haygreen**	Assistant Bar Manager **Samiyat Villegas**	Chief Technician **Michael Paget**	Digital Marketing Officer **Ankesh Shah**
Participation Coordinator **Rach Skyer**	Software Developers **Nick Cripps, Martin Poot**	Health & Safety Manager **Charlotte Croft**	New Work Assistant **Eleanor Dawson**
Sustainability Assistant **Helen Freudenberg**	Individual Giving & Development **Lora Krasteva**	Front of House Supervisors **Emily Jones Mary Roubos James York**	Cleaner **Suber Kemal Sabit**

For a full staff list please see arcolatheatre.com/staff

With special thanks to our volunteers and Supporters

Game Changers
Graham and Christine Benson, Roger Bradburn & Helen Main, Andrew Cripps, Robert Fowler, Daniel Friel, David Alan & Jean Grier, Sarah Morrison, Rosie Schumm

Trailblazers
Katie Bradford, Catrin Evans, Gold Family, Jon Gilmartin, Stuart Honey, Melanie Johnson, Katrin Maeurich

 ARTS COUNCIL ENGLAND Hackney Bloomberg Paul Hamlyn Foundation

www.arcolatheatre.com   020 7503 1646

HOARD

by Bim Adewunmi

∥SAMUEL FRENCH∥

samuelfrench.co.uk

THINKING ABOUT PERFORMING A SHOW?

There are thousands of plays and musicals available to perform from Samuel French right now, and applying for a licence is easier and more affordable than you might think

From classic plays to brand new musicals, from monologues to epic dramas, there are shows for everyone.

Plays and musicals are protected by copyright law, so if you want to perform them, the first thing you'll need is a licence. This simple process helps support the playwright by ensuring they get paid for their work and means that you'll have the documents you need to stage the show in public.

Not all our shows are available to perform all the time, so it's important to check and apply for a licence before you start rehearsals or commit to doing the show.

LEARN MORE & FIND THOUSANDS OF SHOWS

Browse our full range of plays and musicals, and find out more about how to license a show
www.samuelfrench.co.uk/perform

Talk to the friendly experts in our Licensing team for advice on choosing a show and help with licensing
plays@samuelfrench.co.uk   020 7387 9373

Acting Editions

BORN TO PERFORM

Playscripts designed from the ground up to work the way you do in rehearsal, performance and study

---

Larger, clearer text for easier reading

Wider margins for notes

Performance features such as character and props lists, sound and lighting cues, and more

---

+ CHOOSE A SIZE AND STYLE TO SUIT YOU

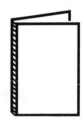

STANDARD EDITION

Our regular paperback book at our regular size

SPIRAL-BOUND EDITION

The same size as the Standard Edition, but with a sturdy, easy-to-fold, easy-to-hold spiral-bound spine

LARGE EDITION

A4 size and spiral bound, with larger text and a blank page for notes opposite every page of text – perfect for technical and directing use

---

MUSIC USE NOTE

Licensees are solely responsible for obtaining formal written permission from copyright owners to use copyrighted music in the performance of this play and are strongly cautioned to do so. If no such permission is obtained by the licensee, then the licensee must use only original music that the licensee owns and controls. Licensees are solely responsible and liable for all music clearances and shall indemnify the copyright owners of the play(s) and their licensing agent, Samuel French, against any costs, expenses, losses and liabilities arising from the use of music by licensees. Please contact the appropriate music licensing authority in your territory for the rights to any incidental music.

IMPORTANT BILLING AND CREDIT REQUIREMENTS

If you have obtained performance rights to this title, please refer to your licensing agreement for important billing and credit requirements.

ABOUT THE AUTHOR

Bim Adewunmi is a producer with *This American Life*. She is a multimedia journalist whose work has appeared in publications such as the *Guardian, BuzzFeed News, Vogue,* and on *Netflix*. Her work was included in the Best American Magazine Writing 2018. She was born in east London and grew upon between London and Lagos. *Hoard* is her first play. She lives in New York.

Photo credit: Sylvie Rosokoff

AUTHOR'S NOTE

Hoard is a specific story, in as much as it is about this one Nigerian-British family in east London. But its heart can also be found in other West African households in London; that same tendency to accumulate, and then the weaving of all sorts of narratives to justify events. The stuffed-full Bakare family homestead in Plaistow is not a one-off; the recollected experiences of the Bakare sisters are not necessarily unique. After all, many of us have our own memories of...*stuff*.

Placing the dinner party in east London was a deliberate choice; while popular knowledge suggests south London as the epicentre of Nigerian life in the capital, east London has long held its own, with thriving Nigerian communities dotted through its postcodes. I'm a proud east Londoner, born and semi-raised there, and it is an integral part of my – and the Bakares' – identity. I wanted to tell this story because the richness of our stories has not always been allowed to exist in public spaces, for public consumption. *Hoard* is both a love letter to east London and also to the many Nigerian-British families who have made a home there. We are *splendid*.

The action takes place in one location: the Bakare sisters' living room-cum-dining room (but it can be extended to include a kitchen if so desired). They are in east London – Dalston or Stoke Newington at a push. This can be a minimalist set: a dining table and four chairs, a sofa, a rug, a tasteful bookcase/shelving with some succulent plants. The actors should feel free to move through the space as the dialogue moves them. This is a small dinner party with a named menu, and food and drink comes up often and joyously throughout the play; it should be served and eaten. For the avoidance of doubt, this is not a family that has hot sauce or even Maggi seasoning on the dining table. The buzzer sound that heralds Wura's arrival must be distinct in its formation, and different to what is heard when Bili and Brian or Ami arrive.

The stage directions are not sacrosanct, but they *are* there to guide the very specific moodscapes the characters occupy over the course of the play. The ellipses, italicised, and bolded words in the dialogue are wholly intentional. When a character's line ends in ellipsis the intention is to trail off, usually awkwardly. Italics denote either a lighter touch in delivery, or emphasis. The bold text denotes a heavier delivery. When the words are both italicised and bold, the actor has the job of emphasising, but lightly. Go with your gut. When a character's words end with --/ they are being cut off, and the next character should start their line with no pause.

It has been my experience in popular culture that African accents of all stripes are treated as the shorthand to a punchline of a joke the author has not necessarily written. That is not to be the case here; for the purposes of performance, only Wura is to have a Nigerian* accent (naturally, after more than thirty years of living in the UK, it will have become somewhat dulled).

*what the ear hears is actually usually a Yoruba accent, but there is sadly little room for nuance in these situations.

FIRST PERFORMANCE INFO

Hoard was originally produced by Avalon and BBC Arts, and previewed at the Bush Theatre on 24 and 25 July, 2018. It featured the following company:

Rafi —Faith Alabi
Ami —Babirye Bukilwa
Bili —Pepter Lunkuse
Wura —Lucy Vandi
Brian —John Omole

Director – Tinuke Craig

Hoard opened at the Arcola theatre on 15 May 2019 with the following company:

Rafi —Elizabeth Ita
Ami —Emmanuella Cole
Bili —Kemi Durosinmi
Wura —Ellen Thomas
Brian —Tyler Fayose

Director – Femi Elufowoju Jr
Stage Manager – Catriona McHugh

ACKNOWLEDGEMENTS AND THANKS

The machine that helped create and bring *Hoard* to life is vast and lovely. My family: Adedayo Adewunmi, Ademola F. Adewunmi, Ade Adewunmi, Demola Adewunmi, Dapo Adewunmi. Karen "HC" Onojaife. Jonty Claypole, Jessi Stewart, Margaret-Anne Docherty, Tinuke Craig, Faith Alabi, Pepter Lunkuse, Babirye Bukilwa, John Omole, Lucy Vandi, Cherrelle Skeete, Tunji Lucas. Margaret-Anne Docherty, Nkenna Ibeakanma, Abby Ajayi, Destiny Ekaragha, Zezi Ifore, Susan Wokoma, the Bush Theatre, Bella Lamplough Shields, Catriona McHugh, Centre 151, ArtsEd, Brooklyn Public Library, every single person at the Arcola Theatre (not least the wonderful cast and director), and of course, every last Nigerian in east London tonight.

*For Ade. I cannot imagine a world without you in it,
because I have never had to*

CHARACTERS

RAFI BAKARE – 29, a classic big sister, intelligent, sharp
AMI BAKARE – 27, a peacekeeper by nature
BILI BAKARE – 24, smart and carefree
BRIAN BURTON – 26, a beautiful, charming American boy
WURA BAKARE – 57, self-assured, formidable,
and comfortable in most spaces

Scene One

Lights up. Friday night, **RAFI** *and* **AMI** *are in their flat, and in their work clothes, still.* **AMI** *is at the dining table.* **RAFI** *on the sofa, enjoying a glass of wine as she marks pupils' workbooks.*

AMI *(musing)* Okay...fried rice: done. Chicken: done. Plantains about to be done. I feel like Nigella Lawson. Only, you know, not rich. And well, *black. (a pause and then as if in realisation)* **Nigeria** Lawson. Imagine?

RAFI *shoots* **AMI** *a brief look.*

Rafi. Rafi, look at me. *(walks over to* **RAFI***)* It would be *amazing.* Picture it: Opening shot, daytime. **I'm dressed in ankara and a cute gele,** [*no not a gele, too formal – a little headwrap so I'm relatable to all the black girls supporting*] cook, serve, fake dinner party.

RAFI *puts down her pen and pays more attention.*

Closing shot: late night, I tiptoe into the kitchen, *wearing an Afrocentric nightie, you know, to startle Bev and Kev of Tunbridge Wells.* **The open fridge illuminates my face, and I open a Tupperware** *- real Tupperware, Raf, not an empty tub of Flora –* and then I eat some food right off of my fingers, before winking at the camera and closing the fridge door.

AMI *looks dreamily into middle distance for a beat.*

RAFI So, what Nigerian food are you licking off your fingers? Because I feel like pounded yam and okra isn't, like, the *sexiest* food.

AMI *(faux-sharply)* Lies! Pounded yam *is* sexy. But fine – there are other sexy foods. We have, um...

RAFI *waits, eyebrows raised, exaggerating patience.*

...Plantains! (AMI *holds a plantain aloft.)* Phallic, because Nigella. But – and this is crucial – it's *actual* finger food.

RAFI Yeah, but dodo is supposed to be hot.

AMI *(massaging temples)* Rafia Bakare, why are you like this? Do you enjoy sprinkling sand in my garri, hm? Stop pissing on my dreams! I could be discovered down Ridley Road market tomorrow! **Nigeria Lawson.**

Extends hand, as if showcasing a cinematic scene.

(in Del Boy Trotter voice) This time next year, Rodders, we'll be millionaires!

RAFI All I know is, you can't put salt on this batch. It's a crime against God and man.

AMI You're just going to have to cope, darling. Because salt on plantains is in keeping with all the tenets of *my* religion.

RAFI News flash: anyone who puts salt on their plantain *has no religion.*

AMI Gerrout of my house, please!

RAFI Abeg – it's my house too! And I can't just idly stand by while you impart faulty wisdom to this un-Nigerian boy, who, by the way, I'm actually excited for you to meet, because I think Bili's fully on board with this one.

AMI Same.

RAFI So imagine Mum goes to visit him and Bili one day, and there he is, sprinkling salt on plantain like a pagan...

AMI *is rolling her eyes at this point.*

...and then the true horror will be revealed: THE CALL!
WAS COMING! FROM INSIDE! THE – *(The buzzer goes
off, cutting* RAFI *off.)* HO-OO-O-USE!

AMI Get the door, weirdo. *(heads into the kitchen)*

RAFI *smiles and walks towards the door. She speaks
lowly into the receiver before pressing the door release
and hanging up. Moments later, the front door opens
to reveal third sister* BILI *and her boyfriend, the guest
of honour,* BRIAN.

BRIAN *is holding a bottle of Prosecco and a shopping
bag containing dessert.*

RAFI You're here! *(yells back to* AMI *in the kitchen)* THEY'RE
HERE!

Come in, come in. *(to* BILI*)* Hello, darling.

RAFI *greets* BILI *and* BRIAN, *taking the bag off him.*

BILI Hey, sweets.

BRIAN Hey, Rafi. How're you doing?

RAFI *(to* BRIAN*)* I'm great, I'm good. How're you doing?

BILI I feel like my stomach is eating itself. When are we eating?

BRIAN I can't wait to eat. *(a pause)* And meet Ami, obviously.

RAFI Well, *obviously.* Don't worry, we'll make you a party
box to go.

RAFI *fusses with the coats, as* BRIAN *starts exploring
the flat and* AMI *emerges from the kitchen.*

BILI *(in a chrirpy Cockney accent)* Awl-right, treacle? *(hugs* AMI*)*

AMI *(hugs* BILI, *tenderly holds her sister's face in her hands,
before kissing her cheeks)* Hello, darling. Food's almost done.

BILI Oh, thank God. *(beat)* Okay, look ferocious, here comes
Brian.

AMI *(turning to* **BRIAN** *with a big smile)* Brian! Such a pleasure to *finally* meet you. *(The two start to shake hands before* **AMI** *shrugs and opens her arms to him in a "ah, why not?" manner.)* I'm gonna hug you. Welcome!

BRIAN Thank you so much for inviting me. Bili tells me all the Nigerian food I've had since I've been in London is trash compared to yours.

AMI Oh, so you're here to do a Yelp review? How *American* of you.

BRIAN *(visibly mildly flustered)* Um, I...

AMI I'm messing with you, Brian. You'll get used to it.

BRIAN *(nervously)* Haha, of course. Um, is there anything we can help with?

RAFI *(gently shooing)* Actually, **you** can tactfully disappear...

AMI Yes, and luckily, we have a task in mind: would you mind popping to the corner shop quickly? We need teabags.

RAFI Yorkshire Tea, please.

BRIAN *(looking at* **BILI** *in realisation)* Ohhh, *sure*. Bili warned me y'all would do this.

AMI Wonderful. So, go. Take your time.

> **BRIAN** *walks away and they all watch him leave.*

RAFI I told you he was cute, didn't I?

AMI You did; he has a real American glow. Clap for yourself.

> **RAFI** *pointedly claps three times.*

BILI *(sighing dreamily)* I think I'm like... **eighty per cent** in love with him.

RAFI Ooh, Bili and Brian, sitting in a tree... *(in a TV news reporter voice, with the wooden spoon as a microphone extended towards* **BILI**) And what do you think will tip the final twenty per cent?

The sisters all pause briefly, thinking.

AMI Ooh, a pregnancy scare!

RAFI *and* BILI *gasp.*

BILI *(shaking her head)* Ami, you play too much! *(a beat)* But, like, *yeah?* *(laughs)* Obviously, I don't *want* to be pregnant. But it **would** give him an opportunity to have the **correct** response to a potentially life-altering situation.

AMI *Yesss.* Like, the church aunties used to say: "Lord, don't send the Holy Spirit to kill him, just shake him small-small!" Nothing bonds a couple like a pregnancy scare. *(a beat)* Or a mugging.

RAFI Wow. So you're both sick. I hate you.

BILI *(in unison with* AMI*)* You love us!

All laugh.

I just mean, I think I'm all the way in with him. We just *fit.* Like we're...just having a natural conversation. You know?

AMI Ugh, okay, budget Neruda.

BILI *sticks her tongue out at* AMI.

RAFI Don't worry, I'm going to keep my game face on. He needs to sweat a little.

BILI *(apprehensively, after a pause)* Guys, do you think it's okay I haven't introduced him to Mum and Dad yet?

RAFI I think it's **very** okay.

AMI I agree. Dad's in Nigeria for the rest of the year, and anyway: where were you going to take him to meet Mum since you can't take him home? Pizza Express? Starbucks? Nah.

RAFI *We'll* do the initial vetting, and only *then* can you ascend to the next level and fight the big boss.

BILI But you don't think th--/

RAFI *(firmly)* No, we do not. The "Plushness of Plaistow" can wait until your one-year anniversary or something.

AMI Yeah, he'll be in too deep by then. And in his confusion that a creature as lovely as you could have emerged from such a hellscape, he'll propose! Ladies and gentlemen, I present to you, the Bakare – *(looks to* **BILI***)* what's Brian's surname again?

BILI Burton.

AMI I present to you the Bakare-Bur—! Wait, you'd be called Bili Bakare-Burton? Triple Bs?

BILI No, I would *remain* Bilqis Bakare. I happen to like my name, thank you very much.

RAFI Right on, sis. *(throws up a militant fist)*

The buzzer goes and **BILI** *goes to answer. Moments later,* **BRIAN** *enters, now bearing teabags.*

Let's eat!

AMI *(to* **BRIAN***)* Get your phone out, Brian – time to start writing your Yelp review.

The group sits down to dinner.

Scene Two

BRIAN Wow, this all looks and smells amazing. I'm in awe of anyone who can cook, let alone cook *well*. *(gesturing)* So, what is all this?

AMI Barely Nigerian, to be honest. *(pointing)* Chicken, plantains. Naija fried rice. I don't mean to brag but my mum says it's the best *she's* ever tasted.

BRIAN Yeah, I had some of her, uh...what was it called again, Bil?

BILI Efo. You had rice and efo.

BRIAN Yeah, that was it. It was *amazing*. My parents are competent, but that's about it. You three must've grown up like royalty, eating all that fine food.

The sisters share a quick, loaded look.

RAFI Sure did. You haven't lived till you've had her pounded yam and egusi.

AMI Yeah, and you *hate* egusi, so that's saying a lot.

RAFI Exactly. Anyway. Time to cross-examine the witness. *(to* **BRIAN***)* In punishingly minute detail, I want you describe *exactly* what you do at your fancy Google job. Follow up: are the office snacks *spectacular*?

BRIAN *(laughing)* They are, actually! And I'm in snack heaven. Right now I'm in love with um ...Bili, what are those salty, melty things called again?

BILI Skips.

BRIAN Skips! I *love* Skips. But um, yeah, my job is essentially a sort of data journalism?

BILI *(proudly)* Brian's team is digitising and analysing the British Library's catalogue. It's a big deal.

AMI So let me get this straight: you work as a tech bro and earn money like a tech bro *(mouths "Right?" to* **BILI***, who nods,* *prompting* **AMI** *to fist bump* **BILI**), but you don't actually have to *be* a tech bro? Wow, Brian, you're my capitalist hero.

BRIAN *(laughing)* I gotta say, I'm kinda my *own* hero, too! I know it sounds boring to a lot of people but I love my job. I have a really amazing team, and getting to move to London, and meeting Bili, and now you guys is...just the cherry on top.

RAFI Brian, you charmer. *(simpers at* **BRIAN** *fake-coquettishly)* I appreciate the attempt but I have to tell you, the only person that needs to hear that flowery shit is Bili.

BILI *(smiling)* Oh, shut up!

BRIAN Okay, so you're a teacher, Rafi, and Ami, you're a freelance journalist. I can't believe how...*spare* this place is. If I were a teacher, there'd be stacks and stacks of crap everywhere. It's bad enough with my own job.

A very brief, almost imperceptible hush falls over the dining table. **BILI** *picks up the rice abruptly.*

BILI Have some more rice, babe.

AMI Yes – eat! I slaved over a hot stove, and I won't rest until everyone's top button is undone. I'm a feeder. I get it from my mama.

BRIAN Wait, so not only is your mum an amazing cook, and she's a feeder too? *(a beat, then to* **BILI**) Did I tell you I don't like my current roommate?

RAFI *drops her fork abruptly, and picks it back up,* **AMI** *gives her a sharp look, while* **BILI** *smiles tightly.*

BILI You don't wanna commute from Zone four, babe, trust me. I mean, yes, you'd get all those amazing meals, but *at what cost*?

RAFI Seriously. Zone two is exactly the right distance for almost everything that matters in London. Believe.

BRIAN *(to* BILI, *fake-exasperated)* I guess I'll just get to know your parents in the more conventional way, then. I mean, I still don't quite understand all the zones on this subway of yours but I can tell you're not joking.

AMI Quite right, Brian. Here at 242 Nuttall Road, we don't believe in jokes and we'll thank you to remember that. Also, promise me you will never in your life call it the "subway" again.

BRIAN *(placing his hand over his heart)* I promise. *(smiling)*

RAFI Okay, I'm just going to go for it. *(in a grand voice)* Brian, I *must* know: what are your intentions towards this genteel creature, our youngest ravishing rose, our Bili?

BILI *(muffled from behind her hands)* Brian, we can leave *right now.*

AMI Hush, Bili. Your presence isn't even technically required. You're lucky we haven't banished you to the kitchen like a housegirl.

RAFI Exactly. Brian, continue.

BRIAN Um, Bili's great, as you know.

AMI That we do, sir. But we're here for *new* news.

BILI *(to* BRIAN*)* Seriously, you don't have to do *any* of this.

RAFI *(mock sternly)* Let him speak, Bil.

BRIAN *(after a thoughtful pause)* I **really** like Bili. And I think Bili really likes me. *(smiles at* BILI, *who smiles back)* And I think it must be going pretty great if I'm getting to meet you two. Cos you three are crazy close – your group chat respects neither time nor place – and Bili would probably dump me the minute we left here if you guys told her to. *(a beat)* Which is why I hope that will not be your recommendation tonight.

RAFI *and* AMI *look at* BILI, *who shrugs slightly.*

AMI *(slow clapping)* Flawless execution. Oh, he's good. Isn't he **good**, Rafi? Triple axel, triple toe loop.

RAFI A bravura performance, Ami, a dream on the ice. He even put his fork down and everything. *(to* **BRIAN***)* Have you done this before, Brian? You've got a gift for it.

AMI You can stay, Brian. Eat some more chicken.

    BRIAN *nods happily, kisses* **BILI** *on the cheek.*

BILI Ugh, I hate you guys.

RAFI *(in unison with* **AMI***)* You love us!

BRIAN So only the parents to go now...

AMI Oh, I'd be careful what you wish for, there, sport – there are always angels listening...

BILI What are you writing right now, Ami?

AMI I'm about to do a pitching workshop for freelance writers. Gonna be super-hard not to just roll up and say: "Don't do it! Go train to be a dentist instead!"

BRIAN My dad's a dentist, actually.

AMI Really?

BRIAN Yeah. He always told me and my sister Karen to run far away from dentistry. He'd say, "Do you wanna spend your entire career staring into people's mouths?" I think he was only half-joking.

RAFI I wouldn't have minded being a dentist, you know. Even with the halitosis exposure. It's a necessary job. *(a beat)* Like hunting.

AMI You *would* say that, Miss I-was-a-school-governor-even-before-I-trained-to-be-a-teacher. You love a boring, necessary job. No offence, Brian. *Some* offence, Rafi.

BRIAN Oh, none taken. My dad would cheer you on.

RAFI Er, I *love* being a teacher. Even if the kids can be little shits. But fine – if I *had* to, my frou-frou career choice would be interior design. I've always loved the blankness of an empty room. Nothing but space to carve up.

BRIAN Well, you've done a great job here. It all matches, but it's not matchy-matchy. And it's sparse but somehow not severe. Which I think is very hard to do.

AMI Oh, there are harder things to do when it comes to interior design, believe me. But thank you.

The sisters share another quick look.

RAFI *(standing up)* Okay, I want cheesecake. Yay or nay? Bili, what flavour—

The buzzer goes off, in a distinct four-piece pattern.

BILI *and* AMI *stand up to join* RAFI, *who is already standing. They look to the door as one.*

BRIAN Are you guys expec—

All three women, without meaning to, hush him in unison, hands flapping impatiently, eyes still focused towards the door.

The buzzer goes again, in the same formation.

AMI I'll answer it. It might not even be...

BRIAN *(to* BILI*)* Might not be who?

BILI It might not be Mu--/

AMI *(goes to speak into receiver and returns quickly)* Yup, it's Mum.

RAFI *(lowly)* Argh, I hate the drive-by visits *the most.*

Scene Three

Enter WURA, *a neat woman with a busy manner. She is carrying three or four bags, maybe one is a "Ghana Must Go" bag. Everyone in the room stands to attention, as though caught doing something wrong.* BRIAN *looks confused by the suddenly rigid atmosphere.*

WURA *E ku'le o!* Hello! Ugh, I'm so tired! *(*WURA *kisses* AMI *on the cheek and continues moving deeper into the living room.)* Where's your sist-- *oh!*

BILI *(rushing forward)* Mum! What a...*bonus* to see you tonight.

RAFI *(pointedly)* You didn't call. *(kisses* WURA*)* I mean, you **never** do, so...

WURA *(with eyes on* BRIAN, *who seems frozen)* Even *I'm* surprised to be here. And you know I can barely use that phone, Rafi. And who is this? *(to* BRIAN*)* Good evening, young man.

BRIAN *(unfreezing)* Hello, good evening! I've heard so much about you, Mrs Bakare! I'm Brian, Bili's bo--/

BILI *(rushing to cut off* BRIAN*)* My *friend*, Brian, Mum! We were just having a nice Friday night dinner. Do you want some rice? Ami cooked. You know you love Ami's fried rice.

AMI I can make you a to-go box, Mum. I cooked so much.

WURA Thank you. But I'm not going just yet. Brian, you don't sound like you're from here. How do you know Bili?

BRIAN Well, Mrs Bakare, we met abou--/

BILI *(cutting* BRIAN *off again)* We met at work. Brian just moved here from California, and he didn't really know anyone in London, so I said he should come round for dinner, and here he is!

WURA That's nice of you, darling, but I was talking to Brian. *(a beat)* Brian?

BRIAN Um, yeah, it's like Bili said, my team... I work at Google, ma'am, and I moved here with my team... I used to live in the Bay Area – that's where my family's from – so this weather's very different, haha! *(a beat)* Anyway, we were doing a book project with Bili's company and she was so great and funny--/

WURA Bili is very funny, yes. She gets that from me. With very few exceptions, the women on her father's side are mostly humourless. *(a beat)* And *short*.

BRIAN Haha, well, Bili's *definitely* funny! Anyway, she offered to show me around and I said yes, and we've been, uh, *friends* ever since? *(looks to BILI)* That's right, right?

BILI *Right*!

WURA Well, that's very nice. One of my favourite Hadiths – do you know, Brian, we're Muslims? Yes, we are – well, one of my favourites is how the prophet, peace be upon him, tells us to feed and to greet those whom we know and those whom we do not know. *(gestures at her daughters)* And look at you, living the Hadith! Wonderful.

AMI *(Upbeat and casual)* That's us, Mum: diligent Muslims, all day, every day. *(slides the bottle of Prosecco out of view)*

WURA And are you American yourself? Or did your parents come from somewhere else recently?

BRIAN Sixth-generation American, ma'am. My sister did some DNA test thing and apparently we have Mali? But I've never done one.

WURA Mali! So we're all West African. Maybe you'd be speaking French or Fula now. Who knows? You know, I speak Hausa myself.

RAFI *(impatiently)* Mum, I thought you'd be home packing for your trip... Or did you finish already?

WURA I *was* packing, but then I went to see Kemi – you remember her? From my old job? Anyway, I told her I was going to Lagos next week, and she asked me if I would help her to take some fabric to her mother, for her younger sister's wedding. So of course, I went to Liverpool Street with her to help her pick colours and patterns. We chose a lovely Hunter green. And I just thought, *let me see these girls on my way home.* And here I am.

BRIAN Well, I'm so glad I got to meet you. I was saying before you got here that I've eaten some of your...what was it again?

BILI Efo.

BRIAN Yeah! Your efo. Delicious. And now I can thank you properly.

WURA You have such nice manners, Brian. You're welcome. If you like, I can make you some again.

BILI Oh, there's no need...

WURA *(sweetly)* Nonsense. There's *clearly* a need. The boy wants efo. I will make him efo.

BRIAN Fantastic! I can't wait.

Everyone looks at their feet for a beat or two.

WURA Rafi, *oya* come and help me unload this. (**WURA** *and* **RAFI** *head into kitchen with a couple of the bags.)*

BILI *(flustered)* Be right back – loo.

BRIAN *and* **AMI** *are left alone in the living room.*

Scene Four

BRIAN So...that's your mom.

AMI Yeah, that's her. *(a beat, then seriously)* Brian.

BRIAN *(just as seriously)* What?

AMI You... are going to see some shit tonight.

BRIAN Yeah, I could already tell.

AMI Well. Just remember--/

BRIAN That I love Bili?

AMI No, just remember that--/ Wait, you *do*? You love Bili?

BRIAN Well, yeah. Of course.

AMI Well, that's a good thing. Have you told her?

BRIAN Not yet. I was gonna say it but--/

AMI But Hurricane Wura made landfall. *(a beat)* Just...*brace yourself.*

BRIAN Oh, um...

AMI Your passport says otherwise, Mum! Brian, could you do me a favour? Could you tip the kettle down the sink? The drain's been a bit slow.

BRIAN *(knowingly)* Oh, *sure!* Not a problem. *(**BRIAN** escapes hastily.)*

WURA *Oya*, Rafi. Back to you. Tell me about all these other men that I, the resident "hard landing", have chased away.

RAFI Delighted to, Mum. Well, there was Alex. Remember him?

BILI *(softly but sharply)* Rafi, please, no...

WURA *(ignoring **BILI**) Enh*, what about him? How am I responsible for breaking him and your sister up?

RAFI I'll tell you, Mum. He and Bili were doing great, and then he saw your house, stacked high and tight with boxes of *varying vintages*, and more or less decided, *"no, thank you"*.

WURA My **stock**? That's what scared a grown man away? *Don't be silly.*

RAFI A version of that "stock" has been in our lives since I was three years old. And I'm twenty nine now, Mum. It may have started out as stock, but it's just "stuff" now. Or worse, unsellable *junk*.

AMI I think what Rafi is trying to say, is th--/

RAFI Ami, I know I'm not the creative writer in the family, but I can still articulate myself quite well, thank you very much.

AMI *(hands raised in surrender)* Oh-*kay*.

WURA *(ignoring **AMI**, speaking to **BILI**)* Did Alex break up with you because of my stock?

BILI *(softly)* Not...*only* because of that. I can see now that we probably weren't perfect for each other. But it's *partly* to blame for why we broke up, Mum, yeah. He wouldn't stop talking about it on the way back. About how he'd never known people lived like that in London, and how he'd seen a documentary about hoarders on Netflix... Anyway, there were lots of reasons for us breaking up. But that afternoon, I just remember feeling so...*ashamed*, Mum. I'm sorry. *(shrug)*

AMI I thi--/

WURA Ami, *please*, stop with your "thinking". Let me hear myself.

BILI And then I watched the documentary, Mum, and the thing is: her house looked like **our** house. It was kind of spooky. It made me think of you, Mum, and it scared me.

WURA *(deliberately)* I don't know what's scaring you, Bili. I have merchandise, and it is earmarked for my customers in Nigeria.

RAFI And you have customers clamouring to buy old newspapers? You're seriously going to ship boxes of them across an ocean, Mum?

WURA Who told you I was going to send the newspapers to Nigeria?

RAFI *You* did. When they *(jerks hand at* BILI *and* AMI*)* tried to put them in the recycling, and you said you had "plans".

WURA So now you give each other reports on "The Woman With The Stuff." Sorry, MI5!

RAFI Ami and I used to joke the flat was like a 3D game of Tetris...

AMI All three of us sharing one bedroom – in a four-bed flat!

BILI When was the last time you were even up in the loft, Mum?

WURA *(looking around at her daughters)* So you're ganging up on me. I pray that your own children will be gentler on you. Amen.

RAFI Oh, amen. *A-MEN*! I'm feeling really prayerful right now too. So! May we have parents who **listen** when their children tell them that their behaviour is making them anxious, and may those parents change their behaviour. Amen. *Can I get an Amen?*

AMI *(more calmly)* No one's "ganging up" – nothing we're saying is new.

BILI Everyone's just trying to figure this out, make sure we're all happy.

WURA I'm happy. I'm **very** happy, actually. So when you say "we", maybe you just mean you and your sisters.

RAFI No, you too, Mum. *(a beat)* Are you *actually* happy living like that? Do you see people's faces when they come over?

WURA *(laughing harshly)* So you want to me to take strangers' feelings into account?

AMI *(quietly)* How about just *ours*?

A beat.

BILI And it's not just strangers. Auntie Sheri loves joking about it.

WURA Sheri isn't *my* family – she's your father's cousin. And she's never liked me. Maybe because she's humourless. *(a beat) And short.*

RAFI Fine – how about Auntie Lola, *your* oldest friend, who's always making snide little comments?

WURA Lola jokes a lot.

AMI *(quietly)* She also tells the truth a lot.

BILI Doesn't it make you a little sad that you can't fully recline in your own house?

WURA I can recline whenever and wherever I want.

RAFI *(changing tack)* So you're going to spend even more money shipping this stuff, when Ami and I could use that money as, oh, I dunno, a deposit on a house?!

WURA It's *my* money, Rafia. **Mine.** I can spend it however I want. And I do not owe you a **single** page from my ledger.

RAFI *(laughing furiously)* So as long as it's *your* money, it doesn't concern us? Wow.

AMI Mum, be honest. Aren't you embarrassed, just a little bit?

WURA Embarrassed about what?

AMI Doesn't it bother you that all of us just stopped bringing any friends round? Since Year 8? You never realise how different you are until an outsider sees it.

BILI Even the British Gas men would look at us funny... I always wanted to shout: we're clean! We don't have rats!

WURA *(slowly looking at her daughters in turn)* Well. I am **so** sorry that the embarrassment of having me as your mother was such a cross to bear all these years. Oh, you *hopelessly traumatised* children! You should have called Childline. Are you all in counselling? Quick, before Theresa May takes away the NHS!

RAFI *(muttering) What the...* Mum! Are you even listening? This has had a direct impact on our lives! Why do you think Ami and I live like this? Maybe we *should* be in counselling! God knows I feel a little bit mad.

WURA You are not mad, by the grace of God! (WURA *looks around in the ensuing silence.)* Oh, we don't say "amen" to prayers any more?

The sisters mumble a subdued "amen".

AMI Mum. You keep sinking money into this "business", and we haven't seen a single return, *ever*. Is it even viable?

WURA You don't know anything about my returns...

BILI Okay, but we're asking about them *now*, Mum.

WURA I'm not going pull out my business accounts to justify myse--/

RAFI *(laughing dismissively)* Of course you're not. You get all defensive and we always back down. Rinse, repeat.

Even Dad's sick of it. *(a beat)* You're a hoarder, Mum. It's a real problem, and I think you're too scared to deal with it.

WURA *(quietly)* Rafia, listen *very* well. Do *not* give me a name my parents didn't give me or one I didn't give myself.

BILI *(placating hands out)* Mum, just watch the documentary. For me. Just consider the possibility that there's a small problem.

RAFI Don't sugarcoat it, Bil. It's more than just a "small problem".

AMI Mum, we found sixteen cases of dried-up Pears soap in the loft last month. We had to throw all of them away.

WURA *(with barely contained rage)* You threw away my merchandise?

BILI Mum, no one was going to buy that.

WURA I still didn't give you the right! How would you like it if *I* came here and threw away *your* stuff?

RAFI That would literally *never* happen, Mum, because we learned from you that the best way to live is to maybe not collect so much stuff? Every decision we have made when it comes to living a good life has been to do the exact opposite of what *you* would do!

The silence is deafening, stretching out while everyone breathes hard. Once again, with exquisite timing, enters BRIAN. *The smile freezes on his lips as he takes in the tense scene.* BILI *raises her hand in his direction as if to physically halt him, and he practically moonwalks back into the kitchen silently.*

WURA Well. I cannot apologise **enough** for all my sins. Sorry to have disappointed you all so much! Even though none of you is God – who is still the only being that can judge me – I **apologise**. *(mock bowing)* I am sorry that my attempts to follow in the footsteps of my own mother, may heaven bless her forever, have been a source of so much...*anguish* for you and your sisters, Rafia.

AMI Mum, everyone's just...frustrated. No one's in anguish.

WURA Oh, I think your sister might be! So check with her before you approach me as the nominated spokeswoman, hm?

AMI We're not trying to hurt you, Mum. But if you won't even acknowledge there's a problem...

WURA There *is* no problem, Amina! Sorry our house isn't *Changing Rooms*. Sorry I'm not Carol Smillie. I don't really care what people think of my house --/

RAFI Clearly...

WURA cuts RAFI a look that silences her.

WURA But let me tell you a few things in the midst of all your *distress*.

The girls are silent, expectant.

How many times has something stored among my so-called "stuff" saved you? Enh? Because when *Mum's stuff* becomes handy, suddenly nobody minds any more, *abi*?

BILI No one's denying there's useful things in *some* of those box--/

WURA Will you let me finish talking? Thank you. Ask Lola. Whose warehouse in Lagos did she visit when she needed help organising her grandfather's funeral? Ask any one of your father's short cousins who they rely on. They'll tell you. **It's me.** Everything has a use, and there's a use for everything.

WURA pauses to collect herself.

I am **not** mad. I am **not** a hoarder.

RAFI God, I wish Dad were here right now. Maybe he could--/

WURA Maybe he could what? You dad is *your* dad, but he's not *mine*.

RAFI Well, I wish your **husband** were here, to say what we sometimes talk about when it comes to your stuff.

WURA Did your fath--/

RAFI *(carrying on)* Cos he talks to *me*, MC Eldest Immigrant Daughter. And that's my other full-time job: talking to Dad about things he should be discussing with *you*.

WURA So you talk about me behind my back? I taught you better manners.

AMI Mum, no one talks about you behind your back.

BILI This is just healthy family stuff.

WURA Thank you, Dr. Bili, so concerned about everybody's health! And does your dad pay for your therapy? Did you make him watch the documentary too? Me too, I've seen documentaries. Are all of you planning an intervention? Or wait, is that what we're doing right now? Is your Dad outside? Are you all going to cry?

RAFI You never take our concerns seriously, do you?

BILI I think we all need to just calm down. We've all had a very long, tiring week, but no one needs to leave here upset.

AMI *(exasperated)* Bil, read the room! This isn't about it being the end of the week, or being tired. This is just another round of a conversation we've been having for twenty years.

BILI *(irritated)* God, you're so condescending.

RAFI *(lowly, to* **BILI***)* She's not wrong, though. *(to the room and* **WURA** *specifically)* It's not an intervention, Mum. I mean, we didn't even know you were coming! But if it looks and sounds like an intervention... Maybe if Dad were here it woul --/

WURA *(clapping sharply)* You can stop right there. You keep bringing up your father like he's a magic key. *(a beat)* What I am to your dad, and what your dad is to me? **That's between us.**

RAFI Well, yes and n--/

WURA Rafia, please! Whatever you talk about with him? That's between *you*. But what is between me and your dad is more than love or habit. You think being in the same house as the two of us means you know how we work? It doesn't! I knew him long before I met any of you. Remember that.

RAFI What's that got to do with--/

WURA I am *begging* you, Rafia. For once in your talkative life, be quiet. The carrot is your love, *abi*? And the stick is that you will report me to my husband - or is he my surrogate dad?

WURA *looks at her daughters in turn.*

Because somehow I seem to have trapped your father in a house of foolish merchandise, *abi*? He is a princess, and I'm the evil hoarding monster. No, not even that. I'm the hoard itself.

BILI *(distressed)* Mum, no one is calling you that...

WURA No, no, no! You can't get shy now. Call me The Hoarder! It's what you've been calling me all night. *(a beat)* Your father and I have our own plans and our own dreams, and my stock - *my "stuff"* - is part of that. And I don't have to explain anything to you. Rafi, you want to talk about jobs? This *(gesturing at the scene)* is **not** my job. You hear me? In fact, I'm tired. I'm going home.

AMI Mum, you don't have to go, please.

RAFI *remains seated, unmoved, slyly observing* WURA's *movements, but saying nothing.*

BILI Mum, please stay. I'll get Brian - you can meet him properly.

WURA *(still collecting her bags)* No, thank you. I'll see him and your children when I get back, - if you feel you can bring newborn babies to a crumbling death shack.

AMI Come on, mum. Please. Don't leave!

> RAFI *continues the mute act. Perhaps she check her nails.*
> AMI, *looks at her, annoyed.*

WURA *(turning back to face the room)* Do you think I like
not selling my stock? You think I don't hear what people
say about me? About my house? You think I'm happy not
to have a business like my mother, heaven bless her? You
girls never think about what failure looks like, do you?
It's easy for you to think about all the ways you have been
inconvenienced, but you don't think about me. I don't own
your lives. But this thing I want for myself – that's why you all
need psychiatric help? I pray to God that your children don't
make you insane like you are trying to do to me. Luckily,
there are no insane people in my lineage, and it won't start
with me. I'm going home.

AMI Mum, *please.*

> WURA, *having picked up all her bags, heads to the door
> silently. We might even hear it shut behind her. As if
> kicked out of a stupor,* AMI *finally moves.*

I'm going to go after her, try and... I dunno! Damage control?
(shouting) Mum, wait! *(She runs out, door slams.)*

Scene Six

BILI Rafi, man. I love you but do you ever just...*stop*?

RAFI What did I do? *She* should stop. I'm just sorry for poor Brian.

BILI *(looks towards the kitchen)* Oh my god, Brian! You're always doing too much when it comes to Mum. Do you know that?

RAFI I *genuinely* do not know what you're talking about.

BILI All of us are in this weird dance with Mum, but no one is dancing harder than you, Raf. *(jerks thumb towards kitchen)* I've got a spooked horse to calm down. *(walks to the kitchen)*

> **RAFI** *shakes her head slightly, as if to shrug off what* **BILI** *has just said. She audibly scoffs, rolls her eyes and picks up her phone before putting it down. After a few more seconds,* **BILI** *and* **BRIAN** *emerge from the kitchen.* **RAFI** *looks up at them, and gives* **BRIAN** *an awkward smile as he sits down.*

RAFI I believe that is known as a baptism of fire.

BRIAN *Yeah...* Look, I hope you don't mind, but I stress-ate at least a third of the cheesecake.

RAFI You know you have to marry Bili now, right? Or we have to murder you.

BRIAN *(laughing)* Well, I didn't come to London to get murdered, so...

> **BILI** *smiles at him.*

Can I just say, it is absolutely *fascinating* to see how other families fight. You guys really...don't hold back, huh. Your mum is terrifying. And funny. It's all very confusing, especially when you're hearing it through a wall.

RAFI Actually, Brian, could you bring the cheesecake in here, please? I need the sugar.

BRIAN *gets up, and starts walking to the kitchen.*

BILI Plates and forks, please! And put the kettle on for real this time?

RAFI *(watching* **BRIAN** *walk away)* I really like him, Bil. Just make sure he doesn't try that *oyinbo* nonsense of calling Mum "Wura."

Both laugh.

Turns out surviving tonight is actually better than a pregnancy scare...

BILI God, were we only joking about that tonight? It feels like forever ago.

RAFI Mum *does* tend to bend the rules of time when she gets going...

BILI *(sighing heavily)* Here you go again...

RAFI I'm going nowhere. Was anything we said here tonight new or revelatory or somehow previously unknown?

BILI That's just a bunch of thesaurus words, and you know it. There's a deeper question for you to answer here.

RAFI Ask away, Riddler. *(folds arms)*

BILI Okay, fine. Have you ever considered *your* reaction to Plaistow?

RAFI Hold on, I'm confused. Somehow we're examining *my* reaction here?

BILI Raf, you were the first to move out. And you *never* moved back.

RAFI What are you saying?

BILI I'm saying that Mum hasn't been the law in your life for more than a decade now. Which means Mum's stuff is just... *not an area of your immediate concern.* But do you see that?

RAFI See what?

BILI *(with exaggerated patience)* Look, it's more than fine to be angry that Mum's stuff made your life unpleasant...

RAFI Well, it *did*.

BILI Raf, I *know*. I was there for most of it too. Remember? I'm on your side, darling.

RAFI *Are* you? You're making it sound like my anger is my own fault?

BILI No, I'm saying that we were all there – we were *all* affected.

RAFI Yeah, but it wasn't as bad for you, was it? Cos me and Ami shielded you a lot. That's the perk of being the baby. You get to live your carefree black girl life while I shout at Mum.

BILI *(mildly sarcastically)* Lucky me. *(a beat)* But – *and don't take this the wrong way* – what are you *still* shouting about? We're all out of that house. So ask yourself: how is it *materially* affecting the quality of your life? In this house, on this day. Right now, Raf – what does Mum's stuff have to do with you?

RAFI A lot.

BILI How?

RAFI *(almost hesitantly)* I know it sounds bananas but Bil, me and her are so alike. What if it's hereditary? What if *I* became like her? *(a beat)* And anyway, we can be upset about things that don't affect us directly.

BILI Or we can choose to rise above it. Like Dad does.

RAFI But it's not like he's happ––/

BILI That's *his* problem! You and Mum were talking about jobs before, right? Well, Dad's given **you** an extra job – he won't confront his wife, but he's more than happy to let *you* do it. No wonder you're so pissed off with Mum – you're carrying rage that doesn't even belong to you.

RAFI tries to interject.

They signed a contract to love one another in sickness and health, and well, maybe this is Mum's "sickness". But we didn't sign a contract, Raf. We *left*. I know it's not the von Trapps escaping the Nazis, but we made it out.

RAFI *(softly, after a pause)* I know, Bili. You think I don't know?

BILI Okay, well. My recommendation? Quit this shitty extra job you never asked for. Look into therapy. Go dancing. *Breathe.*

RAFI It's really hard.

BILI I know.

RAFI I'm just *so* angry with her. All the time. Sometimes, out of nowhere, I'm in the staff room, **seething**. It's making me crazy.

BILI But you can un-crazy yourself. Because it's spilling over. And it will be hard, but you'll be better off. Right?

RAFI Right. You're right.

BILI Well, duh. I may be the youngest, but I'm also the smartest.

RAFI All right, that's enough. You always do too much.

Both sisters laugh.

BILI *(making tea)* Actually, I've been thinking a lot about Mum's stuff recently, especially since we saw those newspapers. And I kept thinking about how many of our Naija friends' parents are in a similar sort of boat.

RAFI Ah, yes. Our Great National Affliction.

BILI No, I'm being serious!

RAFI So am I! It's like a weird sort of...hive mind exoskeleton.

BILI Exactly. All this...*stuff.* Endless stacking. Like the Doozers on *Fraggle Rock.*

RAFI Wow, profound.

BILI Shut up, I *was* being profound! Think of Mum and Dad's whole generation, arriving here with so little, and then they just started...*collecting.* And most of them stopped. But others, like Mum, just never learned how to. Or, maybe they *couldn't.*

RAFI And then I think of Grandma, and how successful *she* was... And I wonder if Mum is chasing that legacy and just never catching up with *her* mum. Like the kids of surgeons who have no aptitude for surgery, and so they're making shit art in Shoreditch? That's how I think of Grandma and Mum. *(a beat)* Only without the shit art.

BRIAN *returns with cheesecake.*

BRIAN Is the tea okay?

BILI It's perfect. Thank you, sweets.

RAFI Yeah, you've really mastered pouring hot water over teabags, Bri. Does anyone call you "Bri"?

BRIAN Not normally. But I'll make an exception for you, Rafi. I feel like you need a clear win tonight. *(BILI splutters, laughing.)*

RAFI *(jaw drops)* Oh, okay, **Bri**. You got jokes!

BRIAN I do!

They all laugh, and drink tea and eat in silence for a couple of beats. BILI *places her fork on her plate deliberately.* RAFI *notices and subtly withdraws.*

BILI Brian, look. This whole...evening was *not* how I wanted you to meet my family. This was a nightmare, to be honest.

BRIAN *(laughs)* Yeah...

BILI You already heard most of it. And I'm sorry you had to see it, but I'm kind of relieved. Because, well, now you know!

BRIAN *(smiling)* Now I know. Ami and I had a little talk earlier, actually - your mum is...she's hard, isn't she?

BILI Just a tiny bit. And I wasn't trying to hide anything but... I like you *so* much, and everything outside of that is *so* messy, and sometimes you just want to...**preserve** the unmessy stuff. Because messes need to be tidied, and I hate tidying. You know?

BRIAN I know. I've been to your flat.

BILI Right. So. I wasn't lying. Just...delaying.

BRIAN *(laughing)* Wow. Forget books – with that gift for spin, Bil, you should be working at the White House...

BILI I'm trying to be serious! Tonight was a lot. But that's my family: a bit shouty, slightly dinged.

BRIAN *(smiling indulgently)* Y'all are crazier than a bag of cats, and I am **legit** scared of your mom. But the thing is... Bili, *I love you.*

BILI *(a delighted pause)* Well, good. Because I love you too.

BRIAN *and* **BILI** *kiss in consummation.*

BRIAN And hey, for all *you* know, my family's issues might make tonight look like a tea party...

BILI Jesus. *(a beat)* I can't wait.

BRIAN Uncle Cyril's a real throwback; he'll probably try to pinch your ass.

BILI I will *break* your Uncle Cyril's hand if he tries anything.

BRIAN Yeah, he'll really enjoy that. He loves a "feisty" woman.

RAFI *returns to the living room.*

RAFI Okay, kids, I need to crash.

BILI *(standing and pulling* **BRIAN** *up)* We should get go—

The buzzer goes off.

It'll be Ami – she probably didn't grab her keys.

BILI *heads to answer the buzzer before getting her coat..*
A few moments later **AMI** *comes into view.*

Scene Seven

BILI Hey, did Mu--/

AMI *(sheepishly and rapidly)* Mum's back!

BILI Oh! Mum, you came back!

WURA Girls. Brian.

Everyone tries to recalibrate in light of **WURA***'s return.*

Bili, will you put the kettle on? I'd love a cup of tea.

BRIAN *(quickly)* Oh, I can make that..?

WURA No, you've already spent too long in that kitchen. *(*WURA *smiles warmly at* BRIAN*.)* Sit down. Tell me more about yourself.

BRIAN Uh, sure. Great.

WURA *(pointedly)* Bili, would you make some tea, please? *(*BILI *heads to the kitchen, bemused.)* Brian, I hope you don't take too much sugar, you know it's bad for you. Do you have any brothers or sisters?

BRIAN Uh, yeah, one sister. She's five years older. She's a doctor.

WURA Wonderful! I thought maybe one of my girls would be a doctor like my brother, but no luck. Rafia, so you're just going to stay silent now?

RAFI Well, no one's asked me a question, so...

AMI Guys...

WURA *(to* AMI*) Which "guys"? (to* RAFI*)* Okay, here's a question: are you going to be angry the whole night?

RAFI I was actually about to go to bed, so no, not the whole night. Just till I fell asleep.

AMI Rafi. Mum. Please.

BRIAN Do you think I should go help Bili...?

WURA *(warmly)* Why? It's tea. She can make it! *(still sweetly)* What do your parents do in California?

BRIAN Uh, my dad's a dentist, and my mom's a music teacher. Piano. She teaches kids, mostly.

WURA How lovely. Bili used to play the drums – she was so good. She gets all that creativity from my side.

BRIAN Oh, I'm sure she does.

WURA Ami, remind me – why did she stop again?

AMI Because she was falling behind at school and you and Dad made her stop her lessons.

WURA *(dismissively)* Is that what happened? I don't remember that at all.

RAFI Yeah, it's amazing what people forget.

WURA *(still pleasantly)* Isn't it? People forget all sorts of things.

RAFI Like what, Mum? What *sorts* of *things* do people forget?

BILI returns from the kitchen with two mugs of tea.

BILI What are we talking about?

AMI Your drumming lessons when you were little. Remember?

BILI Oh, God, yeah. I was pretty good, wasn't I? Maybe I should start lessons again…

RAFI *(to BILI)* You should. It's nice when people get a chance to fix old mistakes.

BILI and AMI eye one another warily.

BRIAN *(abruptly)* I used to play the guitar. Bass guitar.

A couple of beats of awkward silence then, resigned.

Should I just go back to the kitchen?

AMI Brian, stop. Mum, you're off to Lagos soon, and this is **not** going to drag out past tonight. I won't let it. *Okay?* Now, we just spent the last twenty minutes talking about things.

BILI And Rafi and I spent the same amount of time talking here. Right, Rafi?

RAFI Yes.

BILI *(sarcastically)* Okay, **great**. *(to* BRIAN*)* You. Get your coat, love – you've pulled. *(to the rest of the room)* We're leaving. Ami, you wanna walk us to the Overground?

AMI Nothing on earth I'd rather do. Come on, Brian. Chop chop.

BRIAN *(apologetically)* Mrs Bakare, it was *so* great to meet you.

WURA Brian – I'll try and make you some efo before I go.

BRIAN Oh, that'd be great. Enjoy Nigeria, and hopefully see you soon? I mean, it'd be great to see you again. And your husband too. At your hou--/

AMI Time is money, Brian. You'll see Mum again. Let's *go*.

BRIAN Bye, Rafi!

BILI *(all up in* RAFI*'s personal space)* Remember what I said, okay? ***Un-crazy yourself***. It's not your job. I love *you*. *(*RAFI *says nothing but maintains eye contact.)*

I'll call you tomorrow, Mum. Okay? I love you.

BILI *hugs* WURA.

WURA I love you too.

BILI Okay. Train.

BILI, AMI *and* BRIAN *leave, door slams shut. Both* RAFI *and* WURA *flinch slightly at the sound.*

Scene Eight

RAFI *(inhaling deeply)* Okay. Let's talk. I'm going to do my best not to fight with you about this stuff any more, Mum. I don't want to fight, I have **never** wanted this to be a fight. *(through clenched jaw)* I don't. Like. Fighting.

WURA Rafi, I'm not a fighter either. And maybe you don't like fighting with your sisters and your dad. But you've always loved to fight with *me*. You'd screw up your face and make fists and just be ready to fight. You were always a tiny bull. And I was always your red rag.

RAFI Well, I'm not a kid any more. And all of this fighting is making me crazy. *(holds hand up to stop* **WURA***)* Yes, I know we have no crazy ancestors but I'm serious, Mum. I'm tired, and frustrated with you. But I am also making a promise to myself. It's your house, it's your money. It's your...*stuff*. I just have to learn to accept this is something you do, and get over it.

WURA *(scoffing)* Something I do... *(gives* **RAFI** *a considering look)* Do you remember when you were at school, maybe Year 8 or Year 9, and you were interviewed for your school prospectus or something? And they asked you who inspired you as a feminist hero, and you said, *(putting on little girl voice)* "The first feminist I ever knew is my dad." And all the teachers were falling over themselves at your answer, as if you were the first twelve-year-old girl to ever idolise her father.

RAFI *smiles a small smile.*

Yes, you and I can smile about it now. But I was so hurt! Why not *me*? But you and your dad are close; you were always a daddy's girl. Honestly, I don't mind! You are your dad's – I got Ami and Bili. But somewhere along the way you began to weaponise that against me. *(***RAFI** *begins to protest and* **WURA** *holds up a hand.)* And I know! My stuff gets in the way, but you love me, and I love you. We all love one another! But Rafi, you have *always* been fighting me. Nothing I have done has ever made you stop fighting me.

RAFI I don't think that's true at all. Are you really going to say that your hoarding isn't this great, big – sometimes physical! – barrier between us?

WURA Ah *ahn*, Rafia – I *just* said it was! But there are other things at play, and you won't even admit them to yourself.

RAFI *spreads her hands in a gesture of "enlighten me".*

Okay, then. You and your sisters have such a clear idea of what I was supposed to be to you, right? Your teacher, your protector, your provider. Sometimes your friend, or your big sister. Always your mum. And I fulfilled those roles. I even surpassed them. I am a great mother, Rafia. The best. There is nothing I wouldn't do for you...

RAFI Except this!

WURA Rafia! I thought you said you were done fighting?

A beat.

There is nothing I wouldn't do for you three. But Rafi, am I allowed to live my own life during my own lifetime? Am I allowed to have my own dreams? All this "stuff" that you and your sisters dismiss as rubbish, have you ever thought about what it might mean to *me*? All my life, I have put things aside, and I don't regret it: I *wanted* to. I had to. I made my choices, Rafi. And the thing makes you fight me, the thing that made you call your father the first feminist you ever knew, is that you have never really tried to *understand* my choices, or respect them.

RAFI Mum, I respect yo--/

WURA *(laughing softly)* I know you do, Rafi. In your own way. And I respect you back. But you think some of my life choices are *lesser* than your own, and you sit in loud judgement of the things I do, and how I live my life. I know you hate it when I say you will understand more as you get older, but the truth is: *you will*. You and your sisters are always talking about choice and all of that, but you think *my* choices are wrong, and you want to somehow make *me* into *you*. But I am not you, Rafi. You are wonderful, and smart – and tall, like the women in my family (**WURA** *smiles briefly.*) – but I am **not** you. And you are not me.

RAFI But I really don't think that's true, Mum. I don't judge you, I'm just concerned tha––/

WURA What if I told you not to be concerned? Let me worry about me! You have your schoolkids to worry about. Me, I'm a big woman. And my husband is a big man. So stop worrying. Don't be concerned.

RAFI That's really easy for you to say. But, Mum – all that stuff? It's haunted my life. Always looming in the background. A nuisance. And the truth is it *has* made me think twice about bringing people round – not just boyfriends, although yes, boyfriends too. And nothing changes. You just keep doing what you do, and we have no say in the matter. And that's the most frustrating part. *(a beat)* So, no – I don't judge you for not making the same choices I would make. I'm angry because you can see those choices have affectd us and you still don't seem to care.

WURA Ah, Rafia, I *do* ca––/

RAFI And it hurts, Mum. To feel like we don't matter, when we've told you, over and over, that it hurts. It makes me angry, but more than that it hurts me. And Ami. And Bili. And Dad too.

WURA Doing business is hard. It's not as easy as people think. And I am doing it across an ocean. So things are not as smooth as any of us would like. But, Rafi, I get to live my dreams too. *(a beat)* Ask yourself something for me. Will you answer this question honestly?

RAFI *(nodding)* Okay, what?

WURA Besides this stuff, and how it hurt you, is there anything that you have asked me for that I did not do everything in my power to get for you? Think about it: physical things, the things you can't touch. What has been missing from your life that was taken up by my things?

RAFI It's not that simple...

WURA It is! You always wanted to be a teacher. You said it when you were seven years old. You have never changed your mind, not once. And we supported you in every way we could. You became a school governor when you were twenty-one. You did your master's. And now here you are, a teacher. Assistant head of year. Right?

RAFI *nods.*

I never wanted to be a teacher like you. I wanted to have a business like my mother, I wanted to be successful like her, to change people's lives. And all of the stuff – all of my merchandise over the years – all of it was heading towards that. That's my dream. It didn't involve you or your sisters. It was just for me. Before you even existed. So when you and your sisters tell me to watch a documentary about hoarders who have rats and other vermin, I'm the one who's hurt! Did you think about that? About *my* hurt? Or does it not matter as much as yours?

WURA*'s voice has been steadily rising all this time, and now she's standing. The two stare at one another silently, breathing a little hard.*

RAFI *(softly)* I don't know how to fix this, Mum. And I want to fix it.

WURA But there's nothing to fix. It's just the way things are.

RAFI So. What now?

WURA So. We learn to let it go. *(a beat, before she sips her tea)* This tea is cold.

RAFI It was the right temperature when we started this conversation.

WURA Well, it would still be drinkable if you didn't make it like white people. Use condensed milk, instead of cold cereal milk!

RAFI *(muttering) Cereal*--/Do you know how old I was when I realised that we were the only ones at school who called it "cereal milk"? I was ten!

WURA What else are you supposed to call it? It's milk for cereal! What happened to the cans of Carnation I brought here so you can always make my tea correctly?

RAFI Ami baked a really great cake with it, actually.

WURA She's so talented. She gets that from me.

RAFI *(scoffing) Everything* good comes from you!

WURA It's the truth! Speaking of... Do you know who you look like when you're angry?

RAFI Mum, I don't want to kno--/

WURA Like your dad's cousin, on his mum's side. Tola. The one who has two sets of twins. With the eyebrows? Remember? She looks like a monster from one of those cartoons. *(WURA mimes an angry face.)*

RAFI *(stifling laughter)* Mum, you can't say that!

WURA I can, and I did. She always looks like someone woke her up with a slap. And you need to stop frowning so much if you don't want to end up looking like her. Smile. No more fighting.

RAFI I'm trying, Mum.

WURA And that's all I'm asking. *(a beat)* That, and another cup of tea first.

RAFI Fine. I'll go put the kettle on again.

WURA Wait, tell me about this Brian quickly. He's a nervous boy, isn't he? Is that what Bili likes now?

RAFI Mum! I think he only seemed a bit meek because World War Three was happening and he was trapped in the kitchen.

WURA Listen – I don't mind if he's meek. You can get a lot done with a docile man. *(pause for comic effect)* Is he rich?

RAFI Mum! *(a beat)* Yeah, I think he is.

Both burst out laughing.

WURA Good for Bili. We rebuke all paupers, amen? *Amen!*

RAFI *(smiling affectionately, as she exits to the kitchen)* You're ridiculous, Mum.

WURA *(smiling)* I know. Where do you think you get it from?

Lights out.

PROPS

Dining table
Sofa
Glasses of wine
School books being marked
Pen
Door entry receiver
Teabags
Bottle of Prosecco
Shopping bag containing dessert
Wooden spoon
Bowl of rice
Four bags one being a "Ghana Must Go" bag
Mobile phone
Cheesecake
Fork
Plate
Coat
Two mugs of tea

LIGHTING

Lights up (p1)
Lights out (p41)

SOUND EFFECTS

Buzzer (p6)
Buzzer goes off in a distinct four-piece pattern (p11)
Buzzer goes off as before (p11)
Door shuts (p26)
Buzzer goes off (p32)
Door slams shut (p35)

VISIT THE SAMUEL FRENCH BOOKSHOP AT THE ROYAL COURT THEATRE

Browse plays and theatre books, get expert advice and enjoy a coffee

Samuel French Bookshop
Royal Court Theatre
Sloane Square
London
SW1W 8AS
020 7565 5024

Shop from thousands of titles on our website

 samuelfrench.co.uk

 samuelfrenchltd

 samuel french uk